MEDIEVAL BRITAIN

The
Norman
Conquest

Peter Chrisp

Titles in this series:
Life in Medieval Britain
Medieval Monarchs
The Medieval Church
The Norman Conquest

Cover: A carved ivory chess piece of a Norman knight.
Title page: Part of the Bayeux Tapestry, showing Earl Harold of Wessex swearing loyalty to Duke William of Normandy.

Series and book editor:
Geraldine Purcell
Series and book designer:
Simon Borrough
Book consultant:
Dr Lesley Abrams, Lecturer in the Anglo-Saxon, Norse, and Celtic department of the University of Cambridge.

© Copyright 1996 Wayland (Publishers) Ltd.

First published in 1996 by Wayland Publishers Ltd, 61 Western Road, Hove, East Sussex BN3 1JD

British Library Cataloguing in Publication Data
Chrisp, Peter
The Norman Conquest. – (Medieval Britain)
1. Great Britain – History – Norman Period, 1066-1154 – Juvenile literature 2. Great Britain – Politics and government – 1066-1154 – Juvenile literature
I. Title
942'.021

ISBN 0 7502 1743 X

DTP by Simon Borrough
Printed and bound in Italy by G. Canale & C.S.p.A., Turin

Picture acknowledgements

Bridgeman Art Library/British Library 4 (top), 6 (left), 12, 31, 40, 41, /Museé de Tapisserie, Bayeux *title page*, 15, 16, 29, /Richard Philip, London 14, /Pierpoint Morgan Library 23. C. M. Dixon 9, 17, 34. E.T. Archive *cover*, 11, 36. Sonia Halliday 4 (lower), /Laura Lushington 8. Michael Holford 6 (right), 18, 19 (lower), 21, 30, 33, 38, 44. Hulton Deutsch 20, 24-5. Topham Picture Source 26-7, 32, 35, 39. Wayland Picture Library/British Library 7, /Bodleian Library 37, /British Museum 42, 43. All artwork is by Peter Bull.

Contents

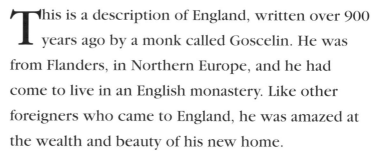

A land of riches and delights

'All earthly riches and delights are found here ... Fields and hills are covered with vegetation, fruits and trees ... There are rich veins of metal: copper, iron, lead, tin, silver and gold.'

Goscelin of St Bertin Acta Sanctorum

This is a description of England, written over 900 years ago by a monk called Goscelin. He was from Flanders, in Northern Europe, and he had come to live in an English monastery. Like other foreigners who came to England, he was amazed at the wealth and beauty of his new home.

Goscelin marvelled at the *'dazzling gold cloth woven by English maidens'*, and the beautiful work of English artists, many of them monks. English churches were full of treasures, such as beautifully painted religious books; and golden boxes, studded with jewels, which held holy relics, such as the bones of saints.

***Above** An illustration for an English calendar, painted around the year 1030, with a farming scene at the top.*

***Right** Many English Bibles were covered with beautifully worked gold and semi-precious stones.*

Different classes

In the eleventh century, the English, or Anglo-Saxons, belonged to different classes. At the bottom were the slaves, people who were bought and sold as goods and who had few rights. Above them were the churls, or free peasants. Higher still were the thanes, or nobles. The most important thanes were called earls. They ruled over great areas of the country, such as Wessex, Mercia and Northumbria, on behalf of the king.

Government

Anglo-Saxon England was a united and well-governed land. The country was divided into areas, called shires, made up of smaller areas, called hundreds. Each hundred and each shire had its own court, which met regularly. It was like a law court and a council.
The king used these courts to set and collect taxes and to call up his army.

The army

In time of war, all free men, such as churls and thanes, might be called up to serve for a limited time in an army, called the *fyrd*. Every shire had to supply a certain number of soldiers, as well as their weapons and money for food.

The king and the earls also had their own full-time warriors, called housecarls. Although they rode to battle, housecarls fought on foot, armed with swords and long-handled battle axes. The English housecarls were said to be the best fighters in Europe.

The ruling earls in 1065

1 Harold
2 Gyrth
3 Leofwin
4 Waltheof
5 Edwin
6 Tostig
  Morcar (from Oct.)

KINGDOM OF SCOTLAND

NORTHUMBRIA
6 • York
• Chester   • Lincoln
5
MERCIA   EAST ANGLIA
WALES   4   2
2   3
• Bristol   • London
            Canterbury •
WESSEX   Winchester
1   Hastings

Map to show English shires in 1065. Also marked are the names of the earls and the areas that they ruled.

English kings

In the eleventh century, England was a Christian kingdom, and people believed that kings received their right to rule from God. It was also thought that a ruler who did not have God's support would bring disaster on his kingdom. God would punish the whole land if he was angry with its king.

Below *Standing between two saints, King Edgar (r.959-75) looks up towards Jesus Christ and the angels.*

The English king was consecrated, or made holy, by the Church in a coronation ceremony. The most important moment came when a bishop poured holy oil onto the king's head. This act was called anointing. It was thought to set the king above ordinary men and women, bringing him closer to God. Britain's kings and queens are still anointed in the same way.

Above *A king of England is crowned by the Church. At the top right, you can see a bishop holding the holy oil, which was used to anoint the king.*

The witan

The king ruled with the help of his witan, or council, made up of leading nobles and churchmen.

The witan also helped to choose a new king. Although being a blood member of the royal family was important, there was no automatic right for the eldest son of the king to be the next ruler. For example, if the king's son was still a child, the witan might offer the crown to a royal stepbrother, uncle or cousin.

When there was no obvious heir, the king might announce that he wanted a particular man to have the crown after his death. This gave the chosen man a claim to the throne. But he still needed the support of the chief nobles. He would not be a true king until he had been anointed by the Church.

Lords and thanes

The word for a noble, *thane*, means *'one who serves another'*. Every thane had a lord whom he had promised to serve. The most important thanes, the earls, promised to serve the king. In their turn, the earls were served by their own thanes. There was a ceremony in which the thane knelt and placed his hands within his lord's hands – by doing this, he became *'his lord's man'*. In return, his lord promised to protect him.

Promises were made binding by the swearing of oaths. These were sometimes taken using holy relics, which were thought to have special powers. The man taking the oath held his hand over the relics and swore: *'By the Lord, before whom these Relics are Holy, I will be loyal and true to* (name of lord) ... *and never, willingly and intentionally, in word or deed, do anything that is hateful to him.'*

Oaths of loyalty were important throughout the Middle Ages. Here King John Balliol of Scotland is promising to obey a later English king, Edward I.

7

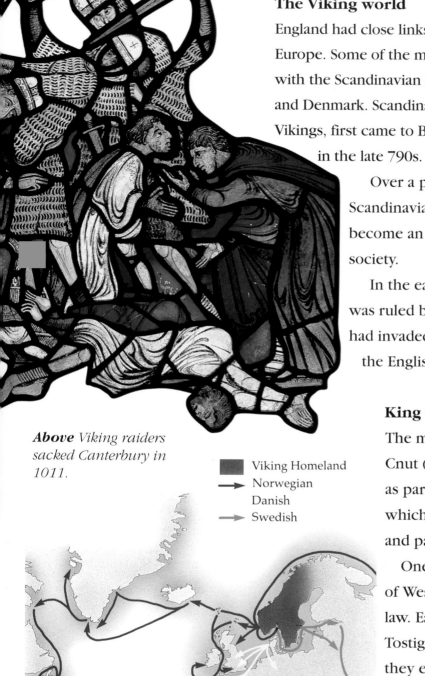

The Viking world

England had close links with other countries in Europe. Some of the most important ties were with the Scandinavian lands, especially Norway and Denmark. Scandinavian warriors, called Vikings, first came to Britain and Ireland as raiders in the late 790s.

Over a period of 200 years these Scandinavians began to settle and become an important part of English society.

In the early eleventh century, England was ruled by Danish kings who, in 1013, had invaded and defeated the armies of the English king, Ethelred (r.978–1016).

Above *Viking raiders sacked Canterbury in 1011.*

Viking Homeland
Norwegian
Danish
Swedish

Routes of the Scandinavian warriors.

King Cnut

The most famous Danish king was Cnut (r.1016–35). He ruled England as part of a great North Sea Empire, which included Norway, Denmark and part of Sweden.

One of the English earls, Godwin of Wessex, married Cnut's sister-in-law. Earl Godwin's sons, Harold and Tostig, were not only half Danish, they even had Danish names. These brothers were to play a big role in English history in 1066 – the year of the Norman Conquest.

Trade

England was busy trading with other lands. There was a constant movement of merchant ships, sailing backwards and forwards across the Irish Sea, the English Channel and the North Sea. This meant that news travelled relatively quickly from one country to another.

Royal City

Winchester was the royal capital, and the place where the king kept his treasure. It was also an important religious centre, with two cathedral churches, the Old Minster and the New Minster, each with a monastery. A third of the city was taken up by palaces and religious buildings.

Towns

Although most English people lived in villages in the countryside, there were also some large towns. The biggest was London, Britain's most important trading centre. It was visited by merchants from France and Germany, bringing wine and fish.

The second largest town was York, here described by an English monk, writing soon after 1000:

'A city well fed and made rich by the wealth of merchants, who come from everywhere, but especially from the Danish people.'

Anonymous
Life of St Oswald

If you visited York in those days, you would have heard Danish being spoken as often as English. Ships from Scandinavia sailed to York up the River Ouse bringing walrus ivory and soapstone, a soft stone which could be carved into bowls.

An English silver penny showing King Cnut wearing a pointed helmet.

The Normans

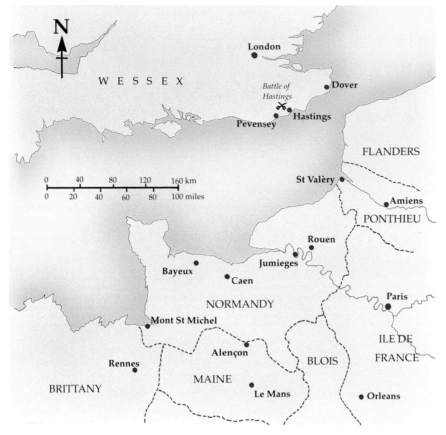

This map shows the duchies of northern France. The area called Ile de France was the King of France's domain. The map also shows how close the English coast is to France. Throughout history there have been periods of war between England and France.

In the eleventh century, France was very different from England. The French king ruled directly over only a small area of land around his royal capital, Paris. The rest of the land was made up of counties, which were small areas ruled by counts, and duchies, which were larger areas ruled by dukes.

The dukes and counts of France were supposed to obey the French king, who was their overlord. But, many of them were powerful and rich in their own right and had their own armies Most of the time, they did what they liked. They were often at war with each other and even with the king. The French dukes and counts built castles to defend themselves against each other's armies. Castles were almost unknown in England at the time.

Normandy and England

England's closest ties were with the duchy of Normandy. King Ethelred of England had married the daughter of the Duke of Normandy (see page 13). When Ethelred lost his kingdom to the Danes in 1013, he fled to Normandy. His son, the future King Edward, was brought up at the Norman court.

Who were the Normans?

Normandy was a relatively new duchy. In 911, the French king, Charles the Simple, had allowed a Viking raider called Rolf to settle on the north coast of France. The king's plan was that Rolf would defend the coast from other raiders. The French called the Vikings 'Normans', or 'Northmen'. The land given to Rolf came to be called Normandy.

Rolf and his Vikings married French women and became Christian. Within a hundred years, the Viking settlers had become part of French society. They stopped speaking Scandinavian languages and were speaking French instead.

From an early age, Norman nobles learned to be expert horseriders, riding and fighting in heavy chain mail. Their war horses were bred to be strong and fast. The Normans trained them not to panic in battle and to turn at a touch of the rider's hand. Norman horses were the best and most expensive in Europe.

The Normans looked different from the English. English men had long hair and moustaches. The Normans were clean shaven and wore their hair closely cropped and shaved at the back. They thought that long hair was unmanly.

Warfare

'The Normans are a race hardened to war, and can hardly live without it, fierce in attacking their enemies, and when force fails, ready to use trickery ...'

William of Malmesbury
The Deeds of the Kings of England
(1130s)

This is a Norman Knight chess piece made about 1190.

William the Bastard

From 1035, Normandy was ruled by Duke William, who was known as 'William the Bastard'. This was because his father, Duke Robert, nicknamed 'the Devil', had not been married to his mother, Herleve. She was the daughter of a tanner (a leather worker).

William did not mind being called bastard. However, he hated being reminded of his mother's humble background. In 1048, the Duke was attacking the castle of Alençon, in Maine. The defenders insulted him by spreading animal skins on their walls and shouting out, *'Hides, hides for the tanner!'* William was so furious that, when he captured Alençon, he ordered that the defenders should all have their hands and feet chopped off.

William's behaviour at Alençon terrified his enemies.

This manuscript illustration shows William as King of England, leading a group of soldiers. From page 14 onwards of this book, you will find out how Duke William of Normandy won the throne of England, and how his invasion in 1066 started the Norman Conquest.

The next castle he attacked surrendered immediately. This was a useful lesson for the duke.

William's early years

William was a hard man, but he had grown up in a violent world. He had become duke at the age of seven or eight. Over the next few years, all four of his guardians died violently, as rival nobles fought each other to get control of the young duke. Some of the nobles hoped to rule through him. Others wanted to kill him and seize the duchy for themselves. As a boy, William's life was often in danger.

The greatest threat came from William's own cousin, Guy of Brionne. In 1047, Guy tried to make himself duke, supported by some of the leading Norman nobles. William, who was about nineteen at the time, desperately asked for help from King Henry I of France. With the king's help, William won a great victory over Guy, at Val-es-Dunes. It was his first battle.

As William grew more powerful, King Henry regretted helping him. The king joined forces with Count Geoffrey of Anjou. In the 1050s, they tried twice to conquer Normandy. Both invasions were defeated by William.

William was a good general and he also had wonderful luck. In 1060, his greatest enemies, King Henry and Count Geoffrey, both died. Their deaths left him free to conquer the neighbouring county of Maine, in 1062–4. In 1064, he also invaded Brittany, and forced the count, Conan, to accept him as his overlord.

By 1066, William the Bastard was the most powerful ruler in northern France.

The family tree showing the link between the English throne and the Dukes of Normandy in the eleventh century.

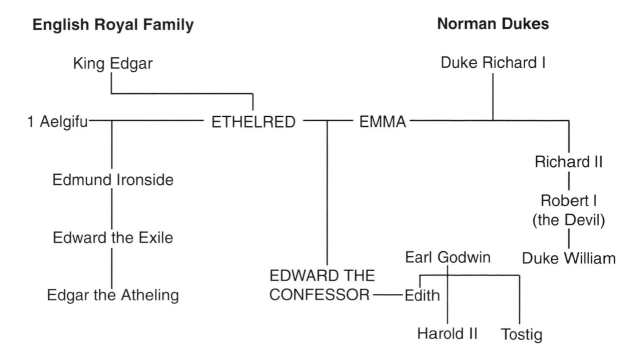

English Royal Family

King Edgar

1 Aelgifu — ETHELRED — EMMA

Edmund Ironside

Edward the Exile

Edgar the Atheling

EDWARD THE CONFESSOR —— Edith

Norman Dukes

Duke Richard I

Richard II

Robert I (the Devil)

Duke William

Earl Godwin

Harold II   Tostig

A fifteenth century painting of Edward the Confessor.

Between 1042 and 1066, England was ruled by Edward the Confessor. He had become King after spending twenty-five years in exile at the Norman court, while England was ruled by Danish kings such as Cnut. Edward was a very religious man, who was made a saint after his death. His nickname, 'Confessor' was a title given to a priest.

On 5 January 1066, Edward the Confessor died leaving no son to be king after him. The only person with royal blood was Edward's great nephew, Edgar the 'Atheling' (prince), but he was still a teenager. Nobody thought that Edgar should be king.

England needed a strong ruler because of the risk of a Scandinavian invasion. The rulers of Norway and Denmark each had their eyes on the kingdom. In 1058, a Norwegian fleet had attacked England, but was driven off. At any sign of weakness, the raiders would be back.

The two rivals

In 1066, two men came forward to claim the crown of England – William of Normandy and Earl Harold of Wessex. In order to find out why they did this, we have to read books written at the time. The problem is that Norman books give a different version of events from English ones. You have to read each version and then make your own mind up about what happened.

The Norman version

According to the Norman writers, Edward the Confessor, who was half Norman himself, loved William like a son. In 1051, he promised William that he would be the next king of England. Then, in 1064, he sent Earl Harold to visit William in Normandy. Harold was said to have sworn an oath that he would help William become king of England after Edward's death.

This was much more than a promise to help William. Harold also accepted William as his lord, whom he was now bound to obey. Disloyalty to your lord was the worst sort of treachery that any noble could imagine.

The day after King Edward's death, Harold was crowned king of England. To the Normans, this speed was proof that he had seized the throne by force:

'This unfeeling Englishman did not wait for the public choice, but breaking his oath, and with the support of a few ill-disposed followers, he seized the throne of the best of kings on the very day of his funeral, when all the people were still weeping over their loss.'

William of Poitiers, **The Deeds of William Duke of the Normans and King of the English**

Harold is shown swearing an oath to William on the Bayeux Tapestry, the famous embroidery which gives us the Norman version of events. You can see Harold's hands outstretched over holy relics.

The English version

English writers saw things differently from the Normans. We can find out the English view thanks to annals, year-by-year histories written by monks. None of the annals mention any promise of the crown made to William by King Edward or Earl Harold.

The most important annals are known as the *Anglo-Saxon Chronicle*. Here is part of a poem from the *Chronicle* describing the death of King Edward:

> *'Yet the wise king entrusted his kingdom*
> *To a man of high rank, to Harold himself,*
> *The noble earl, who ever*
> *Faithfully obeyed his noble lord*
> *In words and deeds.'*

The monks wrote that the dying Edward named Harold, not William, as the next king.

Harold is crowned king of England, on 6 January 1066. William's friends, on the right, are horrified. They will soon be on their way to Normandy with the news.

Harold as war leader

For more than ten years, Harold had been the most important English noble. He was the King's brother-in-law. Harold had already proved his skill as a war leader. In 1063, while Edward was busy building Westminster Abbey, Harold defeated the Welsh in a swift campaign. Harold was the obvious choice to defend England against foreign invaders.

Another monk, John of Worcester, said that Harold had already been helping King Edward rule. He called Harold the 'under-king' :

'After Edward's burial, the under-king, Harold ... whom the king had named as his successor, was chosen king by the chief nobles ... and on the same day Harold was crowned with great ceremony.'

John of Worcester

Annals

According to John of Worcester, Harold did not need to seize the throne by force. The chief nobles in the witan chose him, preferring an Englishman to William, who did not even speak their language.

Harold's new coins showed his portrait. On the reverse a single, hopeful word, Pax *(Peace). There would be little peace in England now that Harold was king.*

Different opionions of Harold

According to the English writers, apart from royal blood, Harold had all the qualities to be a perfect English king:

'Harold immediately began to do away with unjust laws and to make good ones; to pay respect to the Church; and to show himself pious, humble and kindly to all good men. But he treated evil-doers with great severity .... He worked by sea and by land for the protection of his kingdom.'

John of Worcester

The Normans saw Harold in a very different way:
'Harold was stained with vice, a cruel murderer, purse-proud and puffed up with the profits of robbery, an enemy of justice and all good.'

William of Poitiers

The Year of the Comet

At that time, throughout all England, a portent [sign] such as men had never seen before was seen in the heavens. Some declared that the star was a comet, which some call the "long-haired star"; it first appeared ... on 24 April, and shone every night for a week.'

The Anglo-Saxon Chronicle

In the Middle Ages (AD 500–1500), people believed that unusual happenings in nature, such as comets, were caused by God. They were omens, signs that great events were coming.

This comet, blazing across the sky, was also seen in Normandy, where it was described by a writer called William of Jumiéges:

'It lit up the greater part of the southern sky for a fortnight, and many thought that this gave warning of a great change in some kingdom.'

The new comet appears in the sky, watched with alarm by the English. In the borders of the tapestry, below King Harold's feet, you can see the ghostly outline of a fleet. The tapestry makers meant to show that the comet was a sign that vengeance was coming.

William prepares for war

As soon as William learned that Harold had been crowned, he
decided to invade England. Such an invasion was a huge
undertaking for a land as small as Normandy. It took all William's
energy and determination to bring it about. First of all, he had to
win over the Norman nobles.

*'Some of the greatest nobles in Normandy tried to dissuade
him from the enterprise, thinking it to be too difficult and beyond
the resources of Normandy.'*

William of Poitiers

William took his nobles aside, one by one, telling them of the great
wealth that they could win in England. They all finally agreed to back
him, and to provide him with ships, knights, horses and equipment.
Then the duke began to hire knights from the rest of France.

*William's
carpenters
building longships
for the invasion of
England.*

19

A holy war

William also won the backing of the Pope, the head of the Christian Church in western Europe. The Pope gave the duke a special holy banner which he had blessed. The Pope's support meant that the invasion became a crusade, a holy war. This was very important for William's cause. It helped him attract knights for his army from all over France. They believed that they were fighting for God, not just for William. The duke would even go to battle wearing holy relics around his neck.

William clearly believed that Harold had robbed him of his crown. The fact that so many people gave their support to William is strong evidence that he had a just cause. But it must be said that many others simply followed because they would gain lands and wealth if they supported William and he won.

Harold's enemies

Harold knew that he would have to fight to keep his throne, for he had many enemies. Not only did he have William to the south but he also knew that the Scandinavian rulers to the north would take advantage of the unsettled period after Edward's death. Who would be the first to attack, the Normans or the Vikings?

The first blow, which fell in May 1066, came from neither of them, but from Harold's own younger brother, Tostig.

Tostig

Tostig had been Earl of Northumbria, but he had made himself very unpopular there. In 1065, while Tostig was away visiting King Edward, the Northumbrians rose up against his rule. They killed all his followers and seized his treasure. Then they chose a new earl, Morcar, younger brother of Earl Edwin of Mercia.

Once Willliam was king of England he kept his promise to reward his knights with land. Here he is seen handing a land charter to a Norman noble.

Edwin and Morcar raised an army and threatened to invade southern England. They wanted to force King Edward to accept Morcar as the new earl. To avoid a war, the king backed down. Tostig was forced to go abroad to Flanders.

Tostig blamed his brother Harold, who was Earl of Wessex, for not helping him. He also wanted revenge on the Northumbrians. In May 1066, Tostig brought a fleet from Flanders and raided the south coast of England. He then sailed north to Northumbria, where he burned many villages. Driven off by the army of Edwin and Morcar, he went to Scotland, where the king gave him shelter. But Harold had not heard the last of his brother.

Harold defends the south

Harold left the defence of the north to Edwin and Morcar. He believed that the greatest threat was of a Norman invasion in the south. Harold called up the men of the *fyrd*. All along the coast, they kept watch for the Norman fleet. He also stationed his own fleet off the Isle of Wight.

William was stopped from sailing all summer by a strong north wind. It was a tense time for both Harold and William. Each had the problem of keeping his forces together. The men who made up the bulk of each army were only bound to serve for a limited time. They also had to be fed – the delay was becoming expensive.

By September, Harold's supplies had run out and he was forced to send his men home. His fleet sailed to London, many of the ships being wrecked by a storm on the way. This was a great stroke of luck for William.

Just days later, Harold heard more terrible news – this time from the north.

William's fleet was ready to sail from France as soon as the wind changed direction.

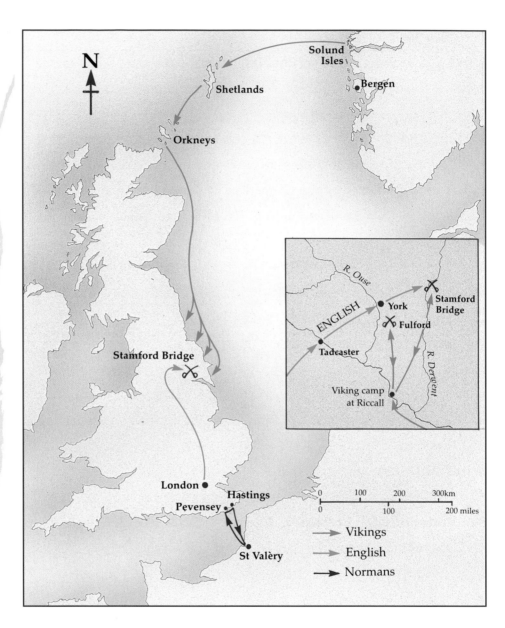

The Norwegian invasion fleet came from the north and followed the English coast down to the mouth of the Humber. Harold and the English army raced north to meet the invasion. Meanwhile, Williams fleet was at StValéry waiting to set sail for the English south coast.

In early September 1066, the people of Scarborough saw a terrifying sight off their coast. A vast fleet of 300 Scandinavian longships was sailing towards them. It belonged to the king of Norway, Harald Hardrada ('hard ruler'). He was a famous warrior, who had spent his life winning battles throughout eastern and southern Europe. Now in his fifties, he was setting out on the greatest campaign of his career, the conquest of England.

22

There were around 9,000 men on board the ships. Apart from the Norwegians, there were warriors from the Orkneys, Shetland and Ireland – all of Scandinavian descent. Tostig was there too, for he had joined forces with Harald of Norway. Tostig had brought a following of Scots and men from Flanders.

The people of Scarborough had no chance against such a huge army. Soon their town was in flames and the fleet was heading south again. After more raids on the coast, the Vikings sailed up the Humber to Riccall, where they made camp.

The Battle of Gate Fulford

On 20 September, Harald of Norway's army marched north to attack York. At Gate Fulford, on the River Ouse, they found their way blocked by a large English army. It was led by Edwin and Morcar.

John of Worcester, the English monk, described what happened when the armies met:

'The English fought so bravely at the beginning that many of the enemy were overthrown; but after a long contest they were unable to withstand the attacks of the Norwegians and fled ... More were drowned in the river than slain on the field.'

A Viking fleet, from a book painted in St Albans around 1130.

Viking victory?

This was Harald of Norways and Tostig's moment of triumph. They had destroyed the English army of the north. As far as they knew, Harold of England was far away in the south, waiting for the Normans. They did not realize that Harold had learned of their arrival, and was racing north with his own army to fight them.

The Battle of Stamford Bridge

On 25 September, Harald and Tostig were at Stamford Bridge on the River Derwent. They had arranged to receive hostages here, from the defeated English. It was a sunny day and the victorious warriors were was feeling very carefree. Then, around midday, their mood suddenly changed:

'They saw a large force riding to meet them. They could see the cloud of dust raised by the horses' hooves, and below it the gleam of handsome shields and white coats of mail .... The closer the army came, the greater it grew, and their glittering weapons sparkled like a field of broken ice.'

Snorri Sturluson,
King Harald's Saga

Right This Victorian engraving depicts the final scene at Stamford Bridge. Harald of Norway is shown in the centre, killed by an arrow. Tostig is also dead, slumped over a fallen horse and with a sword in his hand. King Harold is shown on the right, wearing a crown, grieving over his dead, treacherous brother.

It was the army of King Harold of England, who had rushed north, travelling 300 km in five days. After spending the night of 24 September at Tadcaster, he had quickly marched through York to Stamford Bridge.

The Norwegians had no time to prepare themselves for the surprise attack from King Harold's army. Leaping from their horses, the English housecarls charged down to the river. Waving their swords and axes and shouting their war-cry, *'ut! ut!'* (out! out!), they forced their way across the bridge to Harald's army. In the fierce fighting that followed, both Harald and Tostig were killed.

Harold made peace with Olaf, the son of the Norwegian king. Olaf, who had stayed at the ships during the battle, was allowed to sail home with the survivors. Twenty-four ships were enough to take them back to Norway. Thousands of Scandinavians lay dead at Stamford Bridge, and many Englishmen alongside them.

The *Anglo-Saxon Chronicle* describes the end of the battle:

'The remaining Norwegians were put to flight, while the English fiercely attacked their rear until some of them reached their ships: some were drowned, others burnt to death, and thus perished in various ways so that there were few survivors, and the English had possession of the place of slaughter.'

The Battle of Hastings

Harold had no time to rest or celebrate after his great victory over Harald and Tostig. Two days later, the wind, which had been keeping William from sailing across the Channel, suddenly changed to the east. Now, with Harold still in the north of England, the Normans were at last able to set sail.

On the night of 27 September 1066, William's fleet crossed from St Valéry to Pevensey in Sussex, on the south coast, in the longships packed with knights and horses. There was no one on the coast to stop them landing.

After building a wooden castle at Pevensey, William marched his army east, to Hastings. While some of the Normans were building a second castle here, others scoured the countryside for supplies. They also burned twenty Sussex villages. This was a deliberate insult to Harold, for these villages lay in his old earldom. William hoped to make Harold come south to defend his lands. He wanted to fight a battle as soon as possible.

Right This section of a manuscript illustration shows fully armed Norman soldiers in a longship.

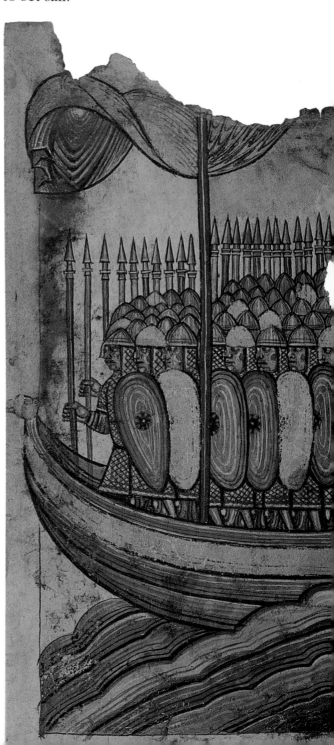

The race south

At the news that William had landed, Harold raced south to London, which he reached on 6 October. Harold now had a choice: he could stay in London, building up a new army; or he could strike quickly with the troops that he had. By waiting, he might force William to move deeper into the countryside, away from his ships, castles and any reinforcements. However, delay would have made Harold look weak. Kings were expected to act decisively, and Harold had to show that he was a true king. So he sent orders to the fyrdmen of Sussex to meet him at the 'hoar apple tree', a well-known landmark just 11 km north of Hastings. It was a mistake to choose a meeting place so close to William's camp. The Normans realized what was going on when they saw English soldiers arriving from all directions.

Harold rode south with his housecarls, hoping to surprise William as he had surprised the Norwegians at Stamford Bridge. But, unlike Harald Hardrada, William knew that Harold was coming.

John of Worcester tells us what Harold decided to do:

'Although he knew well that some of the bravest Englishmen had fallen in the two previous battles, and that one half of his army had not yet arrived, he did not hesitate to advance with all speed into Sussex against his enemies.'

This diagram shows the positions and movements of each army during the Battle of Hastings, 14 October 1066.

The battle

At daybreak on 14 October, Harold was standing on the hilltop by the hoar apple tree, surrounded by his housecarls. As the sun rose, he could see the Norman army, lined up to the south, ready for battle. Harold knew then that he could not surprise William. He would have to fight a different sort of battle from Stamford Bridge.

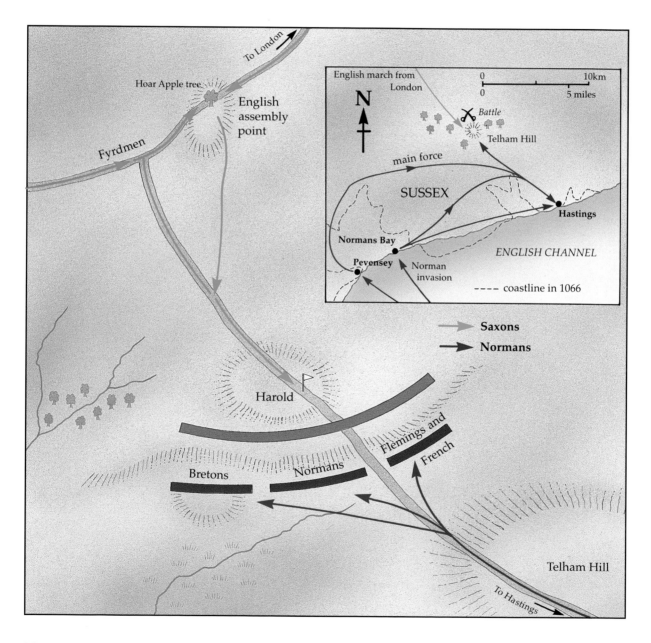

South of the apple tree, there was a high broad ridge. This was the easiest place to defend, so Harold led his men there. They stood close together, protected by a wall of long wooden shields. As they waited to meet the Norman attack, they chanted their war cries, beating their weapons on their shields.

William launched the attack with his archers, but their arrows had little effect against the wall of shields. Then the footsoldiers were sent up the hill, but they were driven back by a hail of stones and spears. Now it was the turn of the Norman horsemen. The Norman knights charged in groups, each following their lord. They found it hard to fight uphill and the English housecarls were more than a match for them.

The Norman knights attack the English shield wall. The dead and dying spill down into the lower border of the tapestry.

29

The English fighters shown here are ordinary fyrdmen, much less well armed than the housecarls in their coats of chain mail.

'For a long time the battle raged with the utmost fury. The English, however, had the advantage of the ground and profited by remaining within their position in close order ... Then the foot-soldiers and the Breton knights, panic stricken ... broke in flight before the English ... and the whole army of the duke was in danger of retreat.'

William of Poitiers

A rumour spread that William had been killed. Hearing of this, he rode among his men shouting, '*I am still alive!*' Encouraged, William's army went back on the attack. According to Norman accounts, they managed to get part of the English army to leave the hilltop by pretending to retreat. As the English followed, the Normans suddenly wheeled their horses around and killed all the English who had been chasing them.

A fourteenth century painting shows William personally killing Harold with his lance. In reality, Harold's death would have been very different, on foot and surrounded by Norman horsemen.

By the end of the day, the English shield-wall was breaking up under the Norman attacks. Harold's brothers, Gyrth and Leofwine, were killed. The King fought on, surrounded by his housecarls. The English monk, John of Worcester, tells us how the battle ended:

'Until dusk he [Harold] bravely withstood the enemy, and fought so valiantly and stubbornly in his own defence that the enemy's forces could make hardly any headway. At last, after great slaughter on both sides, about twilight, the king, alas, fell.'

John of Worcester

Conquering the Land

William had won a great victory at Hastings. Harold and his brothers were dead, alongside the best warriors in the English armies, killed in the three bloody battles of 1066. But William was still not king.

The news reaches London

There was panic and confusion in London when news of the king's death at Hastings arrived. Edwin and Morcar and the other nobles in the witan argued over what they should do. Some wanted to carry on the fight on behalf of Edgar the Atheling, the young prince. But nothing was decided.

Meanwhile, William was waiting at Hastings to be offered the crown by the English leaders. When no offer arrived, he set off with his army. Throughout November, the Normans marched through southern England, looting and burning.

In December, with the Norman army getting closer to London, the English leaders finally made their minds up. They went to meet William and asked him to be king.

On Christmas Day, 1066, William was crowned in Westminster Abbey. Like all English kings, he was anointed with holy oil. This was a moving moment for William, who was said to have trembled violently.

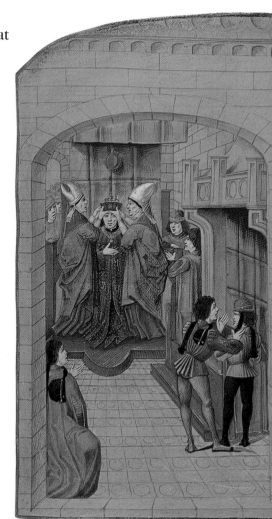

Right This manuscript illustration shows the coronation of William I, also known as William the Conqueror.

Castles

Although William was king, the Normans were still not secure in their rule. They were hated by the English, who outnumbered them greatly. In order to protect themselves, the Normans built castles throughout England. A well-positioned and strongly built castle meant that a small number of Norman knights could control a whole town and usually the whole shire, or county, as well.

The English were forced to help build the castles. This meant several days of hard work, digging a huge circular ditch and piling up the earth into a motte, or mound. On top of the motte, the Normans set up the wooden castle building. At the bottom, they built a bailey, or yard, for stables and workshops.

Castles were put up in around forty English towns. In each town, dozens of houses were pulled down to make room for them. The Normans also cleared space around each castle, to stop their enemies getting too close.

In time, the wooden castles were replaced by stone buildings. As well as being useful for protection, the castles were there to remind the English that they had new, powerful rulers. From the high towers of their castles, the Normans were watching them.

This picture shows Normans building a wooden castle. Before 1066 few English people had ever seen a castle.

'Forming an immense host, riding and marching in high spirits, they all resolutely advanced on York and stormed and destroyed the castle, seizing innumerable treasures, slaying many hundreds of Frenchmen ...'

The Anglo-Saxon Chronicle

William built Corfe Castle to control a large area of Dorset.

Uprisings

Despite the new castles, many English refused to give up the fight. There were several uprisings against Norman rule. In 1071, a southern uprising, at Exeter, was quickly crushed. More serious trouble came from the north in 1069. In January of that year, the English made a surprise attack on Durham, killing the new Norman earl with nine hundred of his men. This was followed by a great uprising on behalf of Edgar the Atheling. The English marched on York and surrounded the Norman castle. William quickly raised troops and rushed north, rescuing his men in York.

In the autumn, there was a second great uprising in the north. This time, the English were joined by a Danish fleet of 240 ships.

For a while, it looked as if William might lose his new kingdom. But he raised another army and rushed back up to York. He paid the Danes to leave. Then he marched his troops through the north. According to the monk, Ordericus Vitalis, William fell on the English 'like a ravening lion':

'In his anger, he commanded that all crops and herds and food of every kind should be brought together and burned, so that the whole region north of Humber might be stripped of all means of livelihood. As a result, a terrible famine fell upon the humble and defenceless people, and more than 100,000 Christian folk of both sexes, young and old alike, perished of hunger ...'

The lands between York and Durham remained almost deserted for fifty years after this harsh treatment by William.

Hereward the Wake

The last place to hold out against Norman rule was the fenland, or wet marshy area, around Ely in Cambridgeshire. This was a place where the Normans could not use their war horses. The men of Ely were led by a thane called Hereward the Wake.

In 1071, William built a causeway, or land bridge, across the fens. His army crossed the causeway and captured Ely, though Hereward managed to fight his way out. No one knows what happened to him, but he became a hero to the English. Long afterwards, they told stories of the adventures of Hereward the Wake.

This tile depicts Hereward the Wake battling with Normans during the uprising and siege of Ely.

Ruling the Land

'The king and his leading men were fond, yes, too fond, of greed for gain. They wanted gold and silver, and did not care how they got it. The king granted his land on the hardest terms and at the highest possible price.'

The Anglo-Saxon Chronicle

The conquest made William enormously rich. The lands which had belonged to Harold and the other English nobles were now his to do with what he liked. He kept much of the best land for himself. The rest was used to reward his followers. The Norman nobles were said to 'hold' the land from the king, rather than own it. They had to pay him rent and services, such as providing him with knights.

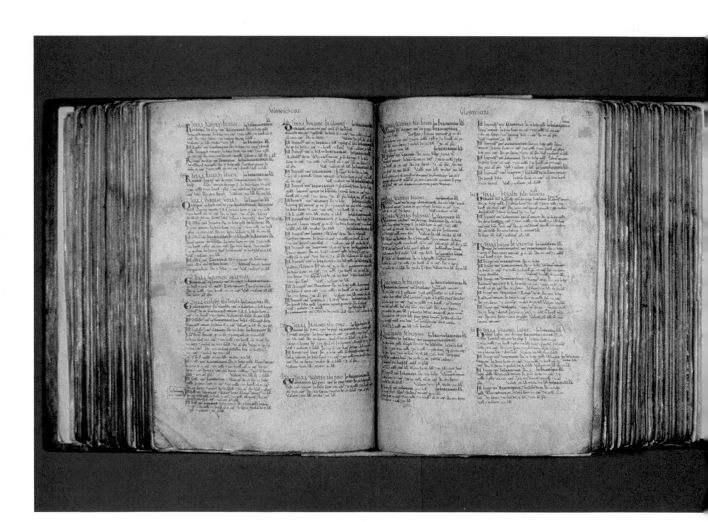

The Domesday Book. William's great survey of England.

Domesday book

In 1086, William ordered a huge survey of England, later called the Domesday Book. Royal officials travelled all over the country, finding out who held land and what they paid for it. The purpose was to make sure that nobody had seized lands that William had not granted them. William also wanted to know whether he could squeeze any more money in taxes out of his people. He needed money to be able to sustain his army, and to reward his followers so he would keep their support.

The survey shows how England had changed in the twenty-four years since the conquest. Thousands of English thanes had lost their lands. Most of the country was now held by 180 French barons. The whole English ruling class had been swept away.

What had happened to all the English thanes?

Many English nobles had been killed in the battles of 1066 and in the uprisings that followed. Others fled abroad, to Denmark, to Scotland and to Greece. Those who stayed behind had to get used to a harder way of life.

'So very strictly did he have it investigated that there was no single hide nor a yard of land, nor indeed (it is a shame to tell it, but it seemed no shame to him to do) one ox nor one cow nor one pig was left out ...'
The Anglo-Saxon Chronicle

Little change for peasants
The lives of the poorest English people, the peasants, were less changed by Norman rule. The churls and slaves continued to work as always, but for new Norman masters, who spoke a different language – French. French was the language of the Court and the Norman aristocracy but it is possible that some Norman barons spoke English to instruct their baliffs and reeves.

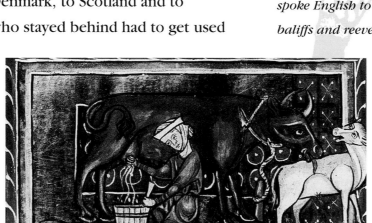

The duties of the peasants changed during Norman rule. This woman is milking a cow while the cow cleans her calf.

Inside Ely Cathedral, one of the vast new churches built by the Normans.

Church building

The Normans used much of their new wealth to build churches. Almost all the old English cathedrals and important churches were pulled down and rebuilt in the grander Norman style. Some of the finest were made using white stone brought by ship from Normandy. Norman lords also built new monasteries, hoping that the prayers of the monks would help the lords get to heaven when they died.

There were different attitudes to the rebuilding. Goscelin, the monk from Flanders who had settled in England, loved the new big churches:

'I hate small buildings; frankly I would not allow buildings to stay standing – even if everyone liked them – unless they were glorious, magnificently big, very tall and spacious and simply beautiful. He destroys well who builds something better.'

But Wulfstan, the English bishop of Worcester, wept when his church was pulled down to be rebuilt. His old church had been small, but it was a holy building, the work of an English saint called Oswald. Wulfstan compared the modern rebuilders with saints like Oswald:

'We miserable sinners destroy the works of saints to win ourselves fame. They never thought to raise great buildings. Instead, they offered themselves to God under any roof, leading all about them by their example. We by contrast labour to pile up stones, neglecting our souls.'

The Normans, who had not heard of most of the English saints, were not worried about pulling down their churches. They believed that small buildings were unworthy of God.

Wulfstan was one of just three English bishops left after 1070. William only appointed Frenchmen to be important churchmen. One reason for this was that bishops were also nobles, who had their own knights. William wanted bishops he could trust.

A holy king

William was a religious man who believed that God had given him his victory at Hastings. He took his role as a consecrated king very seriously. The monks who wrote the *Anglo-Saxon Chronicle* praised his treatment of the Church:

'Though stern beyond measure to those who disobeyed him, he was kind to those good men who loved God. On the very spot where God granted him the conquest of England he caused a great abbey to be built; and settled monks in it and richly endowed [provided for] *it.'*

A statue of William I, on the wall of a Norman Church.

The royal forests

King William had three great interests in life: making money, building big churches and hunting. Whenever he could spare the time, he rode into the woods to hunt deer or wild boar with packs of dogs. He killed the animals with a spear or with a bow and arrow. William also liked hunting wild birds using trained hawks.

England was a wonderful land for a king who liked to hunt. Much of the country was still covered by woodland, which was full of wild animals. William announced that large areas of his kingdom were from then on 'royal forests'. At the time, the word 'forest' meant an area of land set apart for hunting, and forests were protected by special laws. Forests included both wooded and open areas. It should be remembered that most ordinary people lived off the land, not only by farming but, in many cases, by catching wild animals to eat too. Laws which stopped people from hunting were unpopular.

William's forest laws were described in a poem by an English monk:

'Whoever killed a hart or a hind was to be blinded.
He forbade the killing of boars as well as the killing of harts.
For he loved the stags as dearly As though he had been their father.
Hares also, he decreed, should go unmolested.
The rich complained, and the poor lamented,
But he was too relentless to care, though all might hate him...
Alas! That any man should bear himself so proudly
And think himself so high above all other men!'

The Anglo-Saxon Chronicle

William also used the forests to make money. He collected fines from people who broke forest laws. He also charged a fee to farmers in return for the right to graze their pigs on acorns. They were only allowed to do this from late September to November, when the acorns were green and poisonous to deer.

William's death

William died in 1087 but the Norman Conquest of England continued. There were three more Norman kings, and Norman nobles continued to control the English countryside.

The King was not happy with the woodland that already existed. In Hampshire, he cleared farmland and pulled down houses to make a new hunting place. Today, this area of Hampshire is still known as the New Forest.

'After their coming to England, they [the Normans] revived the rule of religion which had there grown lifeless. You might see churches rise in every village … you could watch the country flourishing with renewed religious observance.'

William of Malmesbury wrote these words in the 1130s. Since his readers were Norman nobles and churchmen, he was hardly likely to write that things had got worse under Norman rule. History is usually written by the winners, or by people trying to please them.

Norman influence

Ever since William of Malmesbury's time, writers have been arguing about the results of the Norman Conquest. Writers like Malmesbury believed that the English had been a backward, lazy people who needed the Normans to show them the proper way to live. Other writers say that it was the Normans who were backward. They needed the English royal officials to show them how to rule their new country.

The four Norman kings of England, William I, his sons William Rufus and Henry I, and Stephen, who was the Conqueror's nephew. Each holds the model of a church that he has built.

41

King William's great survey, the Domesday Book, is an example of how people can take opposite views. Some historians say that the survey shows how good the Normans were at organizing and keeping records. Others point out that the survey could never have been made if England had not already been a well-governed land, divided into shires and hundreds, before the Normans came.

Agriculture was important throughout the Middle Ages.

Two languages

One result of the conquest was that England had become a land of two languages. French-speaking nobles ruled over English-speaking peasants. Although William made an effort to learn English, he soon gave up. The Normans looked down on English as the language of ignorant peasants. Those English who wanted to do well, such as the traders in the towns, imitated the Normans by learning French.

Before 1066, all kinds of books had been written in English. The conquest put a stop to this. Poetry would be written in French now; religious books, legal documents and history books in Latin.

Writing in Latin in the 1350s, Ranulph Higden complained:

'Children in school are forced to drop their own language and to learn their lessons in French, and have done so since the Normans first came to England ... and up-country men want to liken themselves to gentlemen, and try with great effort to speak French, so as to be more thought of.'

English comes back

The English language made a comeback in the late 1300s, partly because England was at war with France at the time. English came to be seen as a patriotic language. Writing, in English, in 1385, John of Trevisa commented:

'In all the grammar schools of England, children are dropping French and learning in English .... The advantage is that they learn their grammar in less time than children used to. The disadvantage is that now grammar school children know no more French than their left heel, and that is bad for them if they have to go abroad.'

This illustration shows a monk teaching a class in the Middle Ages. The manuscript is written in Latin, the language of the Church.

The words we speak

The effects of the Norman Conquest are still with us, in the language that we speak. Although English finally won out, it took on many French words. Many of these new words were those to do with power: advise, command, court, govern, parliament, royalty, rule, realm, council. Most terms used in law are also French: judge, jury, perjury, larceny, embezzle. These were the words used by the nobles. There were far fewer borrowings from French in farming or fishing terms.

A silver penny coin showing William the Conqueror.

VENIT:NVNTIVS:ADWIL
GELMVM DVCEM

This section of the Bayeaux tapestry shows an Englishman kneeling in front of a Norman noble. We can tell which figure is Saxon and which is Norman because of the different hairstyles. The Normans brought new fashions, laws and names to the Anglo-Saxon people during the Conquest.

Our names

Names also changed after 1066. The old English ones, like Athelstan, Edgar and Aelfgifu, fell from favour. These sounded odd to the Normans, and the English also began to abandon them. Instead, boys began to be given French names, such as William, Roger, Hugh, Robert, Richard, Geoffrey and Henry; and girls were called Alice, Matilda and Joan. The Normans also liked names from the Bible – John, Stephen, Simon, Matthew, Thomas, Ann, Mary and Elizabeth. The only English name that stayed popular was Edward, because Edward the Confessor was a saintly figure to the Normans.

In the nineteenth century, there was a revival of the old Anglo-Saxon names, such as Alfred, Cedric and Oswald, but this was short-lived. Even now in the English-speaking world, French first names are still more popular than the old English ones.

AD 911	Rolf, a Viking raider, settles in northern France. He becomes first duke of the 'Normans'.
1002	King Ethelred of England marries Emma of Normandy
1013	Following a Danish invasion, Ethelred flees to Normandy.
1035	William becomes Duke of Normandy.
1042	Ethelred's son, Edward, crowned king of England.
1053	Harold becomes Earl of Wessex.
1065	An uprising in Northumbria against Earl Tostig, brother of Harold.
1066	**The invasion**
5 January	Death of King Edward.
6 January	Harold crowned king of England.
May	Tostig raids the east coast of England
20 September	Harald Hardrada of Norway and Tostig defeat the northern English army at the Battle of Gate Fulford.
25 September	Harold of England defeats the Norwegians at the Battle of Stamford Bridge.
28 September	Norman fleet lands at Pevensey in Sussex.
1 October	Harold hears of the landing and marches south to London.
14 October	Battle of Hastings. Harold defeated and killed.
	The conquest
25 December	William crowned king of England.
1067	Rebellion at Exeter crushed.
1069	Two great uprisings in the north of England against William. He puts them down with great brutality.
1071	William captures Ely, the last English stronghold.
1086	William orders a great survey of England, the Domesday Book.
1087	
9 September	Death of William in Normandy.

Glossary

Anglo-Saxons Term used by historians to describe the English people before the Norman conquest.

Anglo-Saxon Chronicle A year-by-year history of England, written in English by monks working between the ninth and the twelfth centuries.

Anointing The application of oil in a religious ceremony.

Bayeux Tapestry A strip of linen, 70 m long, embroidered with pictures showing the conquest from the Norman point of view.

Bishop A leading churchman. He was head of a group of churches, called a diocese.

Cathedral A big church which was also the headquarters of a bishop.

Churls Free English peasants.

Domesday Book A great survey of England carried out in 1086 by William the Conqueror. Domesday means 'Judgement Day', the day when Christ was believed to judge everyone. Legal decisions based on the Domesday Book were said to be just as final as Christ's judgement.

Earl An English nobleman appointed by the king to rule an area of the country.

Fyrd An English army made up of churls and thanes. In time of war the fyrd was called up by the king.

Housecarls Specially chosen fighting men who served a king or an earl.

Hundred An area of England made up, of an area equal to a hundred hides. A hide was a unit of land able to support a single peasant family.

Monk A member of a religious brotherhood living in a monastery.

Relics Things, such as bits of clothing, left behind by Christ or by a saint. Relics were thought to have special powers, such as the ability to cure sickness.

Saints People who had led specially holy lives and who were believed to have the power to work miracles.

Shires Area of England made up of hundreds. It was through the shire court that the king was able to control local affairs.

Thanes English nobles.

Vikings Originally, the word 'Viking' meant a sea raider from Scandinavia (Norway, Sweden and Denmark). The name came to be used in a wider way, to describe the people of Scandinavia between the years 790 and 1100.

Note: The language used in some of the quotations has been changed to make them easier to understand.

Books to Read

The Children's Book of Domesday England, by Peter Bloyden (Kingfisher / English Tourist Board, 1985)
The Normans, by Hazel Mary Martell (Young Researcher series) (Heinemann, 1992)
Norman Britain, by Tony Triggs (History in Evidence series) (Wayland, 1990)
Norman Invaders and Settlers, by Tony Triggs (Wayland, 1992)

Places to visit

Battle Abbey, Battle, Sussex
Tel. 01424 773792
The abbey built by William the Conqueror on the site of his great victory over Harold.

Durham Cathedral,
County Durham
Tel. 01424 422964
The finest Norman cathedral in England

Hastings Castle, Hastings, Sussex
Includes an entertaining audiovisual display, 'The 1066 Story'.

Index

Numbers in bold refer to pictures